T H E HOMESTEAD of WARM SPRINGS VALLEY

VIRGINIA

A PICTORIAL HERITAGE

WARREN & WETMORE
· ARCHITECTS ·
— NEW YORK —

THE HOMESTEAD and WARM SPRINGS VALLEY
VIRGINIA
A PICTORIAL HERITAGE

By Stan Cohen

PICTORIAL HISTORIES PUBLISHING CO., CHARLESTON, WEST VIRGINIA

LIBRARY OF CONGRESS
CATALOG CARD NUMBER 84-60467
ISBN 1-891852-07-8
(Formerly ISBN 0-933126-45-X)

20   19   18   17   16   15   14   13   12   11

Typography: Arrow Graphics
Cover Illustration: Mary Beth Percival
(based on the architect's original rendering)

ABOUT THE AUTHOR

Stan Cohen has authored or co-authored 66 pictorial histories during the past 25 years. He has published over 200 books. Cohen is also the author of Historic Springs of the Virginias, A Pictorial History, which features the historic health spas of Virginia and West Virginia. He is a native of Charleston, West Virginia.

Distributed by:

PICTORIAL HISTORIES DISTRIBUTION
1416 Quarrier Street
Charleston, West Virginia 25301

~§ C O N T E N T S §~

PHOTO INDENTIFICATION

BCHS—Bath County Historical Society
VA—Virginia State Library, Richmond
VHS—Virginia Historical Society, Richmond
VM—Valentine Museum, Richmond
H—Homestead (Virginia Hot Springs, Inc.)

Other photos, maps and drawings not acknowledged are from the author's collection.
Present-day color photographs courtesy of The Homestead. Old postcard views from
author's collection.

❧ I N T R O D U C T I O N ☙

For over two centuries, the secluded, mountain-rimmed Warm Springs Valley of Virginia has rejuvenated the sagging spirits and tired bodies of city dwellers. Before the advent of modern medicine, mineral springs and health spas like those of the Virginias attracted patrons who were eager to "take the cure." Some hoped to alleviate a particular ailment; others came to breathe the invigorating mountain air. During the 18th, 19th and early 20th centuries, entire families would spend a summer at these mountain resorts to escape the heat and disease of the lowlands to the east.

It was during the 19th century that The Homestead began to emerge as one of the most popular of the high mountain spas, and by the 1890s The Homestead was known as a world-class resort. Today, that reputation is undiminished.

Before the white man discovered the spring waters, Indians had frequented the area to rest and to hunt wild game; they, too, were drawn by the valley's tranquility. That tranquility endures, despite a number of disruptions: the Civil War, when troops marched up and down the valley's length; a disastrous fire that engulfed the hotel; the unsettling effects of two world wars and the Great Depression. Through it all, the resort's graciousness and historic charm have prevailed.

In addition to The Homestead, this book traces the history of the other two valley resorts—Warm Springs and Healing Springs. All three resorts are located in Bath County and are owned by Virginia Hot Springs Inc. Most of the story is told through historic and modern photographs. For a more detailed narrative about the resorts, one should read *The Valley Road: The Story of Virginia Hot Springs*, written by former Homestead president, Fay Ingalls.

I wish to thank the management, publicity staff and sales staff of The Homestead for providing information, documents, and historic and modern color photographs. A special thanks for their kind help goes to Dan Ingalls, Jr., president of The Homestead; and John Gazzola, Jr., public relations director. Sepp Kober provided information and photos of his ski operation at The Homestead, and the staff of the Bath County Historical Society was very helpful and provided many photos. Photos also were obtained from the Virginia State Archives, Virginia Historical Society, and the Valentine Museum. Other photos are from the author's collection. Mary Beth Percival did an excellent job on the cover art work. Arrow Graphics typeset the book in ITC Garamond with Schoeffer Initials.

To the resort's visitors: bear in mind that you are following in the footsteps of thousands of guests, some of them very prominent, who in the last two centuries have come to the resort to breathe the mountain air and take the cure, to enjoy the friendly atmosphere and to partake of the resort's social and sports activities. We hope these traditions will continue for the next 200 years.

Now sit back and take a journey into history...

—STAN COHEN

Routes to the springs of Virginia in the early 1800s.

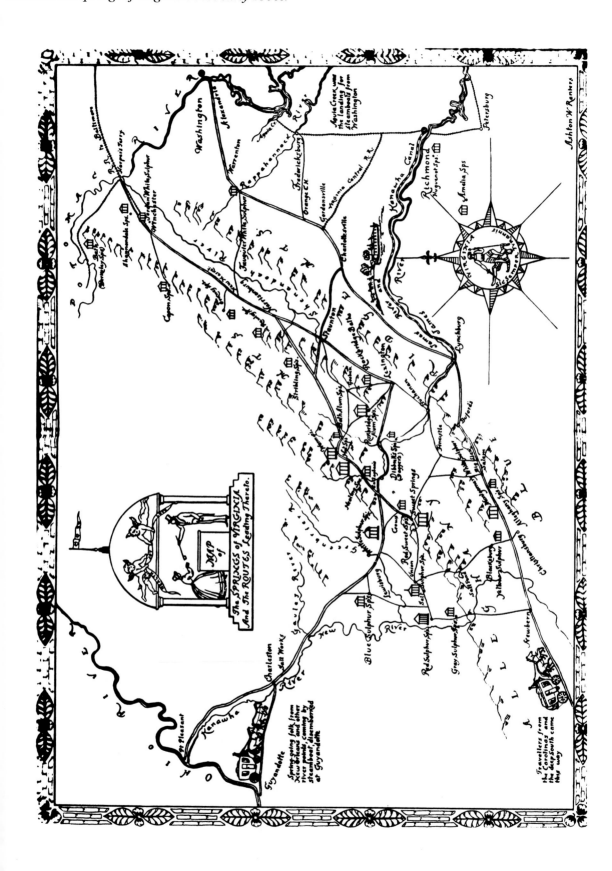

CHAPTER ONE

◦§ E A R L Y   Y E A R S §◦

The recorded history of The Homestead, as well as that of Hot Springs and the Warm Springs Valley, dates back to before the Revolutionary War. Indian legends, however, place the discovery of the spring waters in the 16th century.

A young brave, it is said, was carrying a message from his people in the western valley of the Appalachians to a gathering of other tribes along the ocean shore. After traversing the high mountains for many days, the exhausted brave found himself one evening in a rain-drenched valley that faced an even more formidable-looking mountain range.

At his feet, the weary messenger suddenly noticed the reflection of evening stars in a pool of spring water. He drank from the springs, found the water was warm, and that night slept in the shallow pool. When he awoke in the morning he possessed a new strength. Thus invigorated, according to the legend, the brave hurried to the meeting place on the ocean shore to spread word of his astounding discovery.

The recorded history of the valley starts in the late 1600s when expeditions of white men set out from the Virginia lowlands in an effort to overcome the then-impregnable Blue Ridge Mountains. In 1671, for example, a party traveled as far as the falls of the New River, but could go no farther. By the early 1700s, white men did reach the Warm Springs Valley, and they sought out the warm waters of which the Indians spoke.

The white man's discovery of the actual springs can only be left to conjecture. According to tradition, the discovery was made by Andrew Lewis, who was later to become a famous Indian fighter. It is said that Lewis successfully hid in the springs while being pursued by hostile Indians, although this story cannot be confirmed.

The valley was surveyed between the 1720s and the 1740s and tracts of land were parceled out to what became a colony of Scotch-Irish settlers. At this time Hot Springs was known as "Little Warm Springs" and it was even smaller than the tiny settlement to the north at present-day Warm Springs.

One of the earliest mentions of these settlements is found in the journal of Dr. Thomas Walker, one of the first explorers of Kentucky. Walker wrote in 1750 that the people of Warm Springs were very hospitable but "would be better able to support travelers was it not for the great number of Indian warriors that frequently take what they want from them, much to their prejudice."

Walker also described his visit to Hot Springs: "We went to Hot Springs and found six invalids there. The spring is very clear and warmer than new milk, and there is a spring of cold water within twenty feet of the warm one."

Another early visitor was George Washington. In 1755, Washington, then a colonel of a Virginia regiment, visited the valley while on an inspection tour of forts along the Alleghany frontier.

The first to recognize the potential for a resort at Little Warm Springs (Hot Springs) probably was Thomas Bullitt, an officer at Fort Dinwiddie, located on the Jackson River near the springs. Joining forces with Andrew Lewis and his brother Thomas Lewis, Bullitt in 1764 obtained a deed to 300 acres in the vicinity of the springs.

Soon after, Bullitt bought out the Lewis brothers and in 1766 he built a rustic lodge located on the present Homestead grounds. This was the first hotel at Hot Springs.

Some say it was a small hotel built only after Bullitt had received repeated requests from visitors for lodging and board at his own residence.

It was also in the 1760s that a bathhouse was built at Warm Springs, but business at both spas was slow until the 1790s—until then, the Indian threat had been present and the Revolutionary War had disrupted normal life. While the area was still relatively inaccessible in 1791, the valley's business got a boost from the designation that year of Warm Springs as the seat of newly formed Bath County.

With its location at the county seat, the Warm Springs resort for many years overshadowed the hotel Thomas Bullitt built at Hot Springs. His hotel, the original Homestead, went through a succession of owners and very minimal development until 1832. In that year it was acquired by its first real developer, Dr. Thomas Goode.

A physician from a prominent Virginia family, Goode built the area into one of the dominant health spas of Virginia. He was a good salesman; some might call him a medical huckster. He claimed that the waters of his spa would cure or relieve the symptoms of most diseases.

Goode expanded the resort and in 1846 opened an enlarged hotel built around the original building. Goode built cabins and bathhouses and the resort became one of the premier spas on the region's summer circuit.

By 1838 some 6,000 people were visiting the Warm Springs Valley annually. Yet it was no easy matter to get there. Travelers from Philadelphia and other eastern cities

THE HOT SPRINGS.

The Homestead in an 1857 drawing by Porte Crayon. This was the hotel Dr. Thomas Goode reconstructed about 1846. It stood as is until the major remodeling of the early 1890s. VA

The Hot Springs resort as pictured by Beyer in his 1857 Album of Virginia.   VA

had to undergo a hard four-day journey each way, and no matter where the visitor started, to enter the valley he faced a rough two-day stagecoach trip over deeply rutted mountain roads.

Despite these obstacles, visitors flocked to the valley, attracted mainly by the springs' reputed curative properties. Eventually the journey was eased by steamship service to Fredericksburg and Richmond and rail service that extended partway to the valley. A railroad finally reached the valley in 1892.

After Dr. Goode's death in 1858 The Homestead passed through many hands and development lagged, although the spa still was popular. During the Civil War, both armies marched through the Warm Springs Valley and The Homestead was used as a Confederate hospital. The buildings at all three spas managed to escape destruction during the war.

Following the war, The Homestead again went through a series of owners but it remained one of the dominant spas in the area. In 1890 it was acquired by Col. James A. August and W.S. Edmonds. That same year they transferred the property to the Springs Company on April 14, 1892. After reorganization in 1938, the company name was changed to Virginia Hot Springs, Incorporated.

Hot Springs about 1890. Dr. Goode's Homestead, reconstructed in 1846, is on the left. The three-story brick building in the center probably was built earlier. Also shown are the individual cottages, with bathhouses to the right. At this time there was no village at Hot Springs.   BCHS

This photo was taken about 1892 or 1893, as the large Virginia Hotel, just to the right of the brick building, opened in 1892. The Bathhouse, just in front of the Virginia and partially hidden by trees, also opened that year. Notice that parts of the old bathhouses are gone and the village, in the right background, is beginning to take shape.   BCHS

*By 1893 the Casino, in the right foreground next to the Bathhouse, had been con-
structed and considerable additions had been made to The Homestead.*   BCHS

*View of the back of The Homestead in the 1890s. Cottages 6 and 7, which are now
shops, can be seen in the left foreground.*   BCHS

The Homestead, as reconstructed by Dr. Thomas Goode in 1846, was a magnificent wood structure. This view shows an imposing frontal column porch. The entire building was constructed of wood, heated by open fires, lighted by oil lamps and had very little plumbing. The bandstand on the right was the last structure remaining from Dr. Goode's time. It fell to the wrecking ball in 1966 to make way for the Homestead Club and Grille.   BCHS

Side view of The Homestead, about 1895.   BCHS

CHAPTER TWO

VIRGINIA HOT SPRINGS

◄§ THE MAKING OF A MODERN RESORT §►

The purchase of the Warm Springs Valley's three spas in 1890 by the Southern Improvement Co. led to dramatic changes and expansions.

A syndicate made up of stockholders of the Chesapeake & Ohio Railroad, including Mr. M.E. Ingalls, then president of the line, was instrumental in obtaining the resorts after being rebuffed in trying to purchase The Greenbrier Hotel in White Sulphur Springs, W.Va. The original purchase amounted to 4,700 acres.

A few years after the acquisition, the improvement company merged into the Virginia Hot Springs Co. and the development of the resorts was turned over to Decatur Axtell, vice president of the railroad. Axtell and the new owners lost no time in starting the improvements.

In the early 1890s the company shaped the grounds of the Homestead until they were beautifully landscaped, and constructed miles of drives, riding trails and walks. Ten cottages were built in 1892 at a cost of $17,000 and in 1894 the West Wing was added to the hotel. A six-hole golf course and tennis courts were constructed, and, to upgrade bathing facilities, the company constructed a magnificent stone bathhouse at a cost of $154,000. The Casino, now used as the golf pro shop and dining area, also was constructed at this time.

In 1892, in an effort to make the valley more accessible, a branch line of the C & O Railroad was opened from Covington, Va., 20 miles to the south. This line gave a tremendous boost to the valley's business, and it stayed in continuous use until its abandonment in 1970.

It was also decided that another hotel was needed at Hot Springs, which resulted in the construction of the elegant Virginia Hotel in 1892. The idea was to build the lodging in the style of the European railroad hotels, yet incorporate all the modern conveniences of the day.

The Virginia Hotel, intended to be used in all four seasons, had a few good years while The Homestead was upgraded in the 1890s, but it was plagued by two basic problems. It was situated at too low an elevation, and thus lacked a good view of the surrounding area; it also was located next to the new railroad station, and the coal soot from the engines seeped into the rooms, greatly annoying the guests. Eventually the building's front facade was drastically altered and the hotel was converted into an employee dormitory as well as office and shop space. It is still in use today.

The summer of 1901 saw the end of the old era of the Homestead. At 11 p.m. on July 2 a fire broke out in the hotel's bake shop. Within three hours the entire hotel complex had burned to the ground.

A covered archway connecting the hotel to the Bathhouse was destroyed, saving the Bathhouse, and the Casino and cottages also were untouched. None of the guests were injured, and they found shelter in the neighboring Virginia Hotel and in other area lodgings.

The day after the fire the directors of the Virginia Hot Springs Co. met at Hot Springs and decided to begin reconstruction work immediately. The architects who had renovated the old Homestead were brought in, and on March 10, 1902, the main section of the new Homestead, including a ballroom at the northeast corner, was

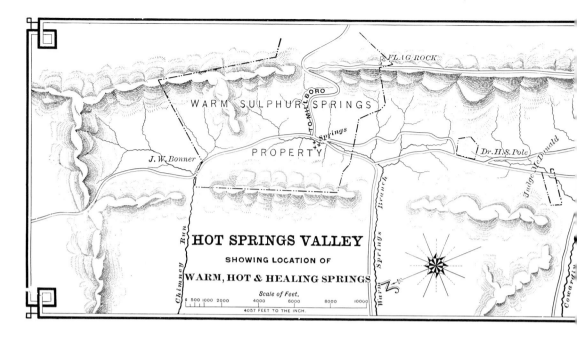

The three properties in the valley owned by the Virginia Hot Springs Co., 1893.

This photo must have been taken in 1892, as the Casino has not yet been built nor additions made to The Homestead. The railroad station and powerhouse, located next to the Virginia Hotel, had been completed. BCHS

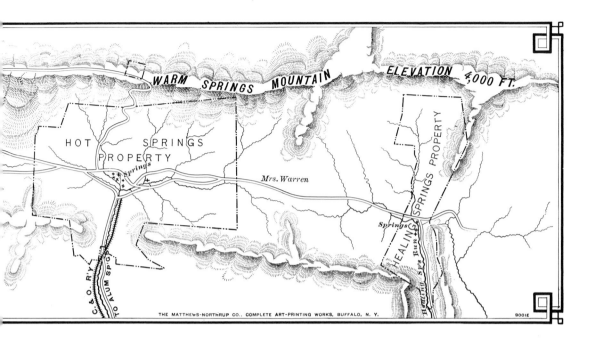

ready for guests. By 1904, the new West Wing, connected to the Bathhouse by a breezeway, was opened. These red brick structures incorporated all the modern fire retardants available at the time—no one wanted a repeat of the July 1901 disaster.

In 1914, the East Wing was constructed in response to the increasing popularity of the resort. By this time The Homestead had become a true world-class hotel in addition to the focal point of the Warm Springs Valley. Although the guests were now arriving from all over the globe, The Homestead management concentrated on preserving the spa's charming colonial atmosphere and traditional Southern hospitality, two features that persist to this day.

The large increase in business prompted other changes. The Homestead developed its own farms and a dairy and poultry business to supply the kitchens. The Healing Springs property also underwent a major expansion. Here, in 1923, the Rubino property and several adjacent farms were purchased for another golf course. East of Healing Springs, on Warm Springs Mountain, a landing strip was constructed. Built in the 1930s, it is now the site of Ingalls Field.

The Homestead's present tower building got its start in 1928 with the commissioning of New York architect Charles Delavan Wetmore. The old 1902 ballroom was razed to make room for the tower, and the million-dollar structure was completed in 1929, just at the start of the Great Depression. The tower greatly increased the capacity of the hotel, but the nation's financial collapse took its toll on the resort's clientele and bookings. The tower had been inadequately financed, and with some 50-year bonds coming due from the 1891 construction, the Virginia Hot Springs Co. was forced into a bankruptcy proceeding in 1938.

Mr. Fay Ingalls, who was president of The Homestead from 1922 to 1957, nursed the resort through the rough years. By 1940, he had reorganized the company into a corporation and put it back on a sound financial footing.

Just when the finances were improving, World War II handed the hotel another setback. Bookings naturally dropped off during the war, and the loss was compounded when Japanese diplomats were interned at the hotel for three months, departing in May 1942. There was some talk of taking over the complex for a military hospital but The Homestead was lucky enough to stay open as a hotel during the entire war, with the exception of the brief Japanese internment. Also during the war, in May and June of 1943, the International Food Conference was held at The Homestead, attended by representatives of the original 44 members of the United Nations.

After the war, business improved steadily. By 1948 the company had undergone another reorganization and the holdings of the railroad had been eliminated. This reorganization greatly improved the tax structure of the company, allowing it to make more improvements to the facilities. Increased business from conferences and conventions led to the construction of the South Wing in 1973. It contains 197 guest rooms and a conference center with a capacity of 1,100.

The Virginia Hot Springs Inc., sold by the Ingalls family in October 1993, had expanded to almost four times the original 4,700-acre purchase made back in the late 19th century. Purchased by Club Resorts, the facilities have kept the traditions and character set forth by Dr. Goode over 150 years ago—the resort offers a world-class facility for business or pleasure.

Servants on the porch of the Homestead, late 1890s.   BCHS

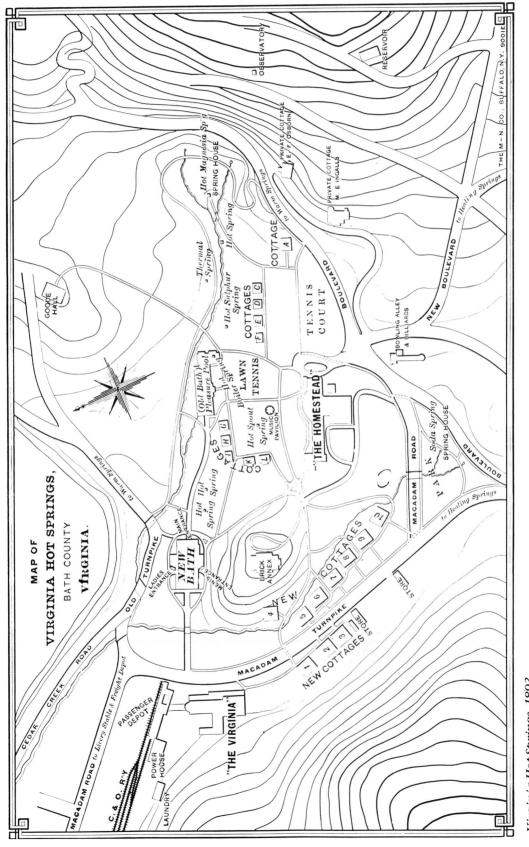

MAP OF
VIRGINIA HOT SPRINGS,
BATH COUNTY
VIRGINIA.

Virginia Hot Springs, 1893.

By 1894 the original West Wing, which extended toward the Bathhouse, was completed and an enclosed archway connected the two. The village is taking shape in the background.   BCHS

View of the back side of the hotel 1894.   BCHS

Another view of The Homestead and new West Wing, Bathhouse, Casino, old bath-houses and Virginia Hotel in the background. Circa late 1890s. BCHS

The Casino, constructed in 1893, with the Octagon Spring in the foreground. The iron fence has been replaced by concrete balusters. BCHS

The Homestead in the late 1890s. The present building now occupies this site.   H

The stately Virginia Hotel in the early 1900s. Several alterations can be seen in this view when compared to the photo on the top of the next page.　　　VHS

Once the railroad arrived at Hot Springs, a new hotel, the Virginia, was built in the style of the European railroad station hotels. It was soon discovered, however, that the hotel was situated too low in the valley for a good view and the belching coal smoke from the train irritated the guests. Constructed in 1892, it was later converted to other uses. The front facade has since been greatly modified. BCHS

Although the old Virginia Hotel is still an imposing structure in the village of Hot Springs, it has been stripped of its former elegance and most of its original front facade. It is now used as a dormitory, store and office space. H

The branch line of the Chesapeake & Ohio Railroad from Covington to Hot Springs was completed in 1891 and covered a distance of 20 miles. Trains arrived every day and made the resort accessible to all parts of the East. Passenger service was terminated in 1970 and the last freight train ran on Nov. 30, 1973. The station has since undergone considerable alterations. The field in the foreground is now the site of the village of Hot Springs.   BCHS

The Adams Express office at the Hot Springs railroad station, 1893. This was replaced by the American Express Company, then the Railway Express Agency.

BCHS

The old Homestead livery stables, located in Hot Springs. The stables burned down many years ago.   BCHS

Magnesia Springs springhouse, on The Homestead grounds, at the end of the East Wing.

Cottage Row in 1893. Ten "modern" cottages were built at a cost of $17,000. The Soda Springs springhouse is seen in the center. This photo was taken from the front of the Virginia Hotel.   BCHS

Four of the original cottages built in front of the original Homestead, sometime before The Civil War. A lawn tennis court can be seen in front.   BCHS

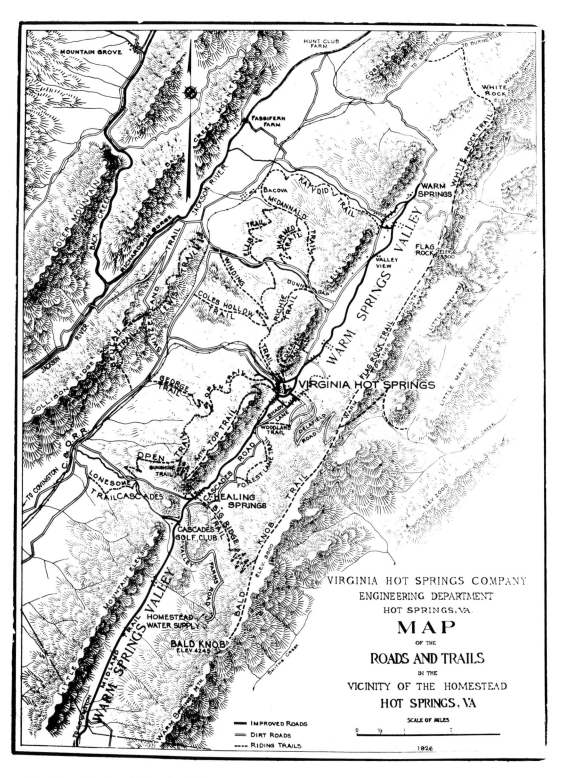

The Warm Springs Valley in 1926.

On July 2, 1901, a fire that supposedly started in the hotel's bake shop completely destroyed The Homestead. There were about 100 guests in the hotel but all escaped uninjured. Although the fire was a disaster to the Virginia Hot Springs Co., the company immediately started planning for a new building. BCHS

A new, brick hotel rose from the ashes in 1902. The main section, including a circular ballroom, was completed in March of that year. The extension along the crest of the hill that is known as the West Wing was completed in the fall of 1903. The East Wing, connected to the ballroom, was completed in 1914.   BCHS

Formal gardens, 1920s. The new South Wing is now located in this area.   VA

LOBBY OF THE HOMESTEAD HOTEL.

The main lobby of the new Homestead, early 1900s.   BCHS

The new Homestead's veranda, now the main entrance. VHS

Luncheon on the lawn near the Casino. VHS

Top: In 1928 a major expansion was started with the construction of the present-day tower. The 1902 circular ballroom was torn down to make way for the construction.   H

Bottom: The tower was nearly complete when this photo was taken in March 1929, just before the Depression hit.   H

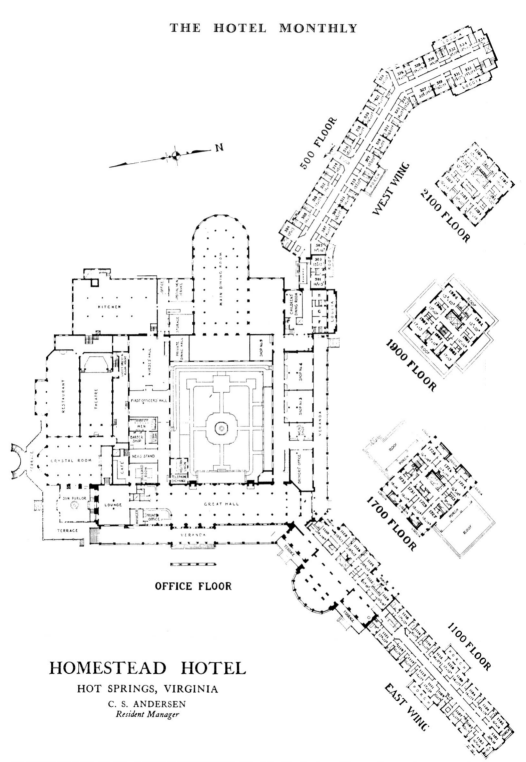

HOMESTEAD HOTEL

HOT SPRINGS, VIRGINIA

C. S. ANDERSEN
Resident Manager

GROUND FLOOR PLAN of THE HOMESTEAD, Virginia Hot Springs. Changes in recent years are at once seen by comparing the ground floor plan printed in The Hotel Monthly of July, 1921. The Tower section has replaced the former ballroom. It is indicated on the plan by the section connecting the Great Hall with the East Wing. Other changes will be noted in the south side of the main building in the section devoted to Sun Parlor, Crystal Room, Theater and a la carte Restaurant. The Terrace bordering the Sun Parlor and Crystal Room and the dining room overlook a colorful and perfectly kept garden centered with a fountain and lily pond. (Inserts show plans of different levels in the TOWER. Note the private porches for suites.)

Main entrance to The Homestead, 1930s.   VA

Back side of the magnificent tower and East and West wings with the Sulphur Spring in the foreground.   H

CHAPTER THREE

❧ENJOYING THE GOOD LIFE❧

Simple relaxation has always been a high priority for The Homestead's guests. Even in the early days, when many visitors came to the Spa in hopes of curing an agonizing ailment, guests made an effort to partake of the good life. This especially was true in the 1800s when traveling to the valley was a real hardship.

Since the time of Dr. Goode's tenure, every possible comfort has been afforded the guests. To this day, for example, the hotel carries on the old tradition of afternoon tea in the Great Hall.

In the old days, as now, there was no lack of diversions from a spartan health routine. These included billiards and bowling, both extremely popular, as well as horseback riding and pleasure excursions in buggies and carriages. For some, strolling the spacious grounds was pleasure enough, and in the evening, of course, there was eating and drinking in addition to dancing to the hotel's fine house bands.

After the 1890s, tennis and golf became the resort's two most popular activities, a position they hold today. Yet the modern Homestead offers more than sporting and leisure activities. It also provides facilities to conduct meetings and hold large conventions for academic, business, professional and fraternal organizations.

Gen. George C. Marshall, former Army chief of staff and U.S. secretary of state, visiting The Homestead with Mrs. Marshall. H

Cordell Hull, secretary of state during World War II, at The Homestead.
H

Over the decades, The Homestead has hosted scores of prominent people and famous politicians. Former presidents who visited The Homestead while in office were William Howard Taft, Woodrow Wilson, Calvin Coolidge and Lyndon B. Johnson. Other politicians who visited included Franklin D. Roosevelt, while governor of New York, and, when they were vice presidents, Richard Nixon, Spiro Agnew, Gerald Ford and Nelson Rockefeller. Ronald Reagan has visited The Homestead, as did Dwight Eisenhower, though neither was in office at the time.

Other names that have appeared on the hotel's guest list are Vanderbilt, Phipps, Kennedy and Mellon, in addition to the Duke and Duchess of Windsor, Gen. and Mrs. George C. Marshall and Cordell Hull. During the 1930s New York socialite Mrs. Cornelius Vanderbilt used the resort as her summer retreat.

In the more distant past, The Homestead received frequent visits from Thomas Jefferson, Robert E. Lee and possibly George Washington.

The good life goes on ... enjoyed by people from around the globe.

A wedding party on The Homestead grounds, circa 1905.   BCHS

Garden Room, 1920s.   H

Crystal Room, 1920s.   H

Lobby of the new tower, circa 1930. H

Smoking and card room. This was removed in 1927 to make room for the new tower. H

Dining room, circa 1930s. H

The Japanese Room, once one of the more exotic sections of The Homestead. The room no longer exists. H

Years ago an annual waiters' tray race was held on the Casino lawn of The Homestead. The event has since been discontinued. H

The Homestead

BREAKFAST

A LA CARTE
PER PERSON

Cover Charge 15 (Including Rolls, Toast and Butter)

FRUIT

Compote of Stewed Fruits 75   Stewed Fresh Pears 75   Sliced Bananas with Cream 40
Grapefruit, (half) 50   Pear 30   Fresh Strawberries with Cream 75   Orange 25
Apple Sauce 30   Baked Apple with Cream 40   Stewed Prunes with Cream 45
Sliced Oranges 50   Tomato Juice 40   Grapefruit Juice 50   Sour Crout Juice 50   Orange Juice 40

PRESERVES

Blackberry   Strawberry   Raspberry   Peach 30   Figs 50   Strained Honey 45   Comb Honey 45
Orange, Grapefruit or Grapefruit-Cherry Marmalade 30

CEREALS

All Cereals with Cream 50

Shredded Wheat   Cream of Wheat   Puffed Rice   Grape Nuts   Oatmeal
Corn Flakes   Yellow Corn Meal Mush
Post Toasties   Krumbles   Health Bran   Wheatena   Hominy Grist

CAKES, ETC.

Old Fashion Virginia Waffles with Maple Syrup 70
Wheat, Rice or Indian Cakes with Syrup 50   Fried Hominy 60   Fried Yellow Corn Meal Mush 60

EGGS & OMELETTES

Boiled 50   Au Beurre Noir 60   Shirred 70   Benedict 1.00   Fried 50   Florentine 1.00   Scrambled 60
Bacon and Eggs 1.00   A la Turque 1.00   Poached 70   Ham and Eggs 1.00   Poached with Bacon 1.00

OMELETTE- Plain 70   Fine Herbs 1.00   Chicken Liver 1.00   Spanish 1.00   Jelly 1.00
Ham 1.00   Cheese 1.00   Kidneys 1.00   Tomato 1.00   Mushrooms 1.00

FISH

Clam Broth 50   Panfish Saute Meuniere 1.00
Kippered Herring 1.00   Codfish Cakes 1.00   Broiled or Boiled Salt Mackerel 1.00
Broiled Fresh Fish 1.00   Creamed Salt Codfish 1.00

MISCELLANEOUS

Lamb Hash, Green Peppers 1.25   Broiled Canadian Bacon 1.00   Broiled Bacon 90
Corned Beef Hash with Poached Egg 1.00   Lamb Kidney Broiled or Saute 1.00
Veal Kidneys with Bacon 1.25   Broiled Honey Comb Tripe 1.00   Calfs Liver and Bacon 1.25
Broiled Pig's Feet 1.00   Beechnut Bacon 1.00

Chicken Hash with Poached Egg 1.50

Homestead Sausage Cakes 1.00   Broiled Ham 1.00

STEAK, CHOPS & HOMESTEAD POULTRY

Steak, Minute 1.75   Pork Chop 1.25   Veal Chops 1.25   Filet Mignon 1.75
Tenderloin (for one) 2.00   Broiled Loin Lamb Chops 1.25   Lamb Chops 1.25

Broiled Farm Chicken (Half) 1.75

POTATOES

Baked 40   Hashed Brown or Saute 50   French Fried 50   Lyonnaise 50   Hashed in Cream 50

COFFEE

Percolator Per Person 35 Extra   Pot 25   Tea 25   Cocoa 25   Milk 15   3-21-30-20

BREAKFAST MENU of the a la carte dining room, The Homestead, Virginia Hot Springs.

Leisure-time activities, early 1920s.

1950s.

The children's playground opened in 1955.

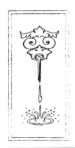

CHAPTER FOUR

◦◦ W A R M S P R I N G S ◦◦

Warm Springs, the county seat of Bath County, is located five miles north of Hot Springs, and was once the site of a very popular resort. Today, not much remains of the resort, but the springs are still in use.

The Warm Springs, as their name suggests, are slightly cooler than the Hot Springs. They have a water temperature of 98 degrees and contain a larger variety of minerals than the other springs in the valley.

According to legend, the Warm Springs pools were discovered by an exhausted Indian runner in the 16th century. Visitors were drawn to the valley's springs as early as the mid-18th century, and in 1751 a 140-acre tract that included the present Warm Springs was surveyed for Thomas Lewis and his son John. The younger Lewis settled the land and died there in 1788.

In 1761, the Men's Pool and Bathhouse was constructed. Still standing, it is one of the oldest spa structures in existence in the United States. It is not quite as large as the adjacent Women's Pool and Bathhouse, which was built in 1836. The Men's Pool is octagon in shape, 40 feet in diameter and 120 feet in circumference. It can hold 43,000 gallons of 98-degree water. The Women's Pool is circular, 50 feet in diameter and 150 feet in circumference, and the water temperature is a little less than 98 degrees. In the Women's Pool, a crude lowering device, reportedly installed for use by Mrs. Robert E. Lee, is still in existence. It is a chair on a platform that was lowered by a windlass into a

Beyer's rendering of Warm Springs from his 1857 Album of Virginia.   VA

spring-fed pool just off the main pool. The springs supplying these pools contain nitrate, calcium, iron, chloride, bicarbonate, sodium and sulphate deposits.

The first substantial structure built in the area apparently was the Colonnade, a hotel three stories high with a narrow terrace in front from which huge columns rose to a projection of the roof. It could have been constructed as early as 1810-12. A larger "E"-shaped hotel was built a few years later. Like the Colonnade, it was three stories high, and it contained only one bathtub and had two large outside toilets. When cottages were added to the complex it could house more than 300 guests.

Many prominent people patronized Warm Springs, including Alexander Hamilton, Robert E. Lee and Thomas Jefferson, who spent considerable time at the resort. Back then, visitors commonly bathed in the pools twice a day, remaining in the water from 12 to 20 minutes each time and avoiding active exercise while submerged. It was thought that the best times for bathing were before breakfast and dinner.

The spa attained its height of popularity in the years preceding the Civil War. At the time it was owned by John Brokenbrough, who operated the resort from 1828 until 1852. After the war, Hot Springs became the most popular spa in the valley and the visitation at Warm Springs declined rapidly.

Warm Springs' last individual owner was Col. John L. Eubank, secretary of the Virginia Secession Convention of 1861. The Warm Springs assets were purchased by a syndicate in the 1880s, but Mrs. Eubank continued to operate the hotel under lease. After her departure, the company leased the hotel to others and then for some years tried to operate the resort with a manager. It became a money-losing venture, however, and in 1924 the hotel was closed. The hotel, the Colonnade and most other buildings were razed a year later.

All that remains today of this once-fashionable resort are several cottages, one supposedly built before 1800, and the two bathhouses. Virginia Hot Springs Inc., which owns the bathhouses, still opens them to the public during the season.

These stately buildings at Warm Springs stood until 1925, when they were torn down due to decay. The Colonnade building, in the left background, was built about 1810-12. The Warm Springs Hotel, on the right, was built a few years later.

WARM SPRINGS.

Warm Springs, from an 1883 Baltimore & Ohio Railroad booklet.   VA

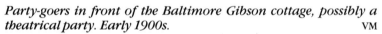
Party-goers in front of the Baltimore Gibson cottage, possibly a theatrical party. Early 1900s.   VM

The front porch and large columns of the Warm Springs Hotel, early 1900s.   VM

Cottage Row at Warm Springs, early 1900s.   VM

LADIES' BATH,

WARM SPRINGS, BATH COUNTY, VIRGINIA.

---

50 feet in Diameter. Warm Sulphur Water, 98° temperature.

THE WARM SPRINGS

ARE NOW OPEN AND WILL BE

KEPT OPEN EACH YEAR UNTIL AFTER OCTOBER 15th.

The above is a correct view of the Ladies' Bath. The Gentlemen's Bath is a similar one, only not quite so large. There is a flow of SIX THOUSAND gallons of Warm Sulphur Water per minute.

The BATHS are said to be the FINEST IN THE WORLD.

The internal use of the water, conjoined with the Baths, has been found signally beneficial in the following diseases:

CHRONIC AND SUBACUTE RHEUMATISM AND GOUT,
NEURALGIA, PARALYSIS, DYSPEPSIA,
(especially that form connected with disturbance of the Liver or a torpid state of the bowels,)
DISORDERS OF THE URINARY ORGANS,
CHRONIC DISEASES OF THE SKIN,
ALL DISEASES OF THE BLOOD,
AND THE DISEASES PECULIAR TO FEMALES.

PASSENGERS FOR THE WARM SPRINGS GET OFF AT MILLBORO' DEPOT.

Apply to the proprietor of hotel at that place for transportation. He will furnish comfortable carriages and baggage wagons at moderate prices. Stage Coupons received.

JNO. L. EUBANK, *Proprietor.*

288½ SEND FOR PAMPHLETS.

-53-

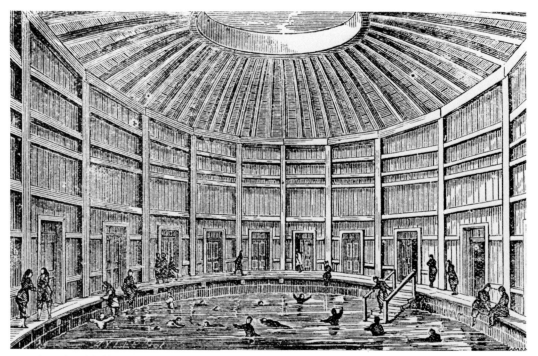

A rather idyllic interior drawing of the Women's Pool, from an 1881 Chesapeake & Ohio Railroad directory.   VA

Present-day interior view of the Men's Pool.   VA

Women's Pool.   VA

The Women's Pool and Bathhouse, built in 1836 and still in use. The circular structure is 50 feet in diameter and the pool holds 60,000 gallons of slightly less than 98-degree water. BCHS

The Men's Pool, built in the 1760s and one of the oldest such structures in the country. It is an octagon 40 feet in diameter and its pool holds 43,000 gallons of 98-degree water.

One of the original Warm Springs cottages, still in use. It is thought to have been built in the 1760s and is located near the old hotel site.

CHAPTER FIVE

❧ H E A L I N G   S P R I N G S ❧

Of the three major spas in the Warm Springs Valley, Healing Springs, located two and one-half miles south of Hot Springs on U.S. 220, has been the least developed.

As late as the 1850s, the area was of a primitive appearance, as noted by Dr. William Burke, the well-known proprietor of Red Sulphur Springs, who also urged the development of Healing Springs. The area, wrote Burke, is "as rude and wild as nature can make it. If improved with judgment, and rendered accessible by turning the great western road that way, which can easily be done, it will prove a great acquisition to the neighboring group of resorts and especially to the Hot Springs, and will rapidly grow into favor with those for whom the waters of its class are appropriate."

It is believed that the development of Healing Springs began about the time of Burke's writings, though it is not known who developed the area or built the first hotel. Cottage Row, which was torn down in 1975, is said to have been built in 1856, and the large Healing Springs Hotel existed at the time of the Civil War, when it was used as a Confederate hospital.

The hotel, except for its dining facilities, apparently was torn down sometime before 1893. The former dining hall became a fancy finishing school for young women in the early 1900s, and is now the Cascades Inn.

Two separate springs, Healing and Little Healing, serve the area. Both are thermal and have the same mineral content. Healing Springs, along with other properties in the valley, was acquired in 1890 by the Virginia Hot Springs Co., which still owns it today. Little Healing Springs was purchased in 1895 by Jakey Rubino, a trader on the New York Stock Exchange.

Rubino changed the name to "Rubino Healing Springs" and began marketing bottled spring water. The Virginia Hot Springs Co. instigated litigation to stop him from using the word "healing" in his advertisements, as the water was determined to have no curative properties. Rubino finally won the case, but by that time the popularity of bottled water had declined.

Rubino's property was purchased by the Virginia Hot Springs Co. in 1923 for expansion of its golf facilities, and the large home he had built there was remodeled into a golf clubhouse. The Cascades Course opened in 1924 and the clubhouse—the Cascades Club—is still in use today.

Healing Springs played a minor role during World War II when the Cascades Inn was used to intern the ambassador from Vichy, France, and his staff after they had complained about their accommodations at Warm Springs. Today, guests who stay at The Homestead can use all the facilities at Healing Springs, which include the Cascades Inn and two golf courses.

BALL ROOM.   REAR VIEW O

L.   DINING HALL.

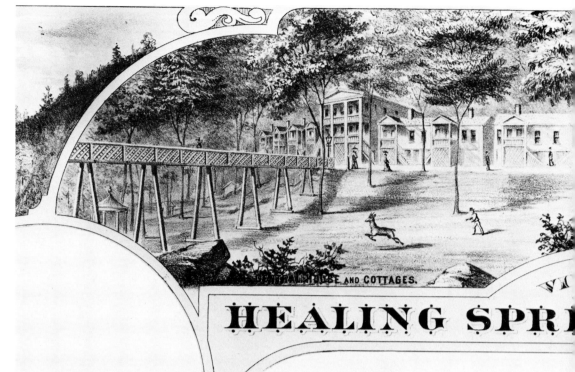

CENTRAL HOUSE AND COTTAGES.

HEALING SPRI

GENTS

LADIES

BATHING HOUSES AND COTTAGES.

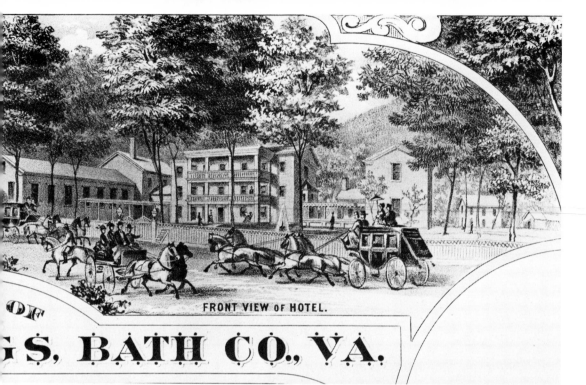

FRONT VIEW OF HOTEL.

GS, BATH CO., VA.

SPRING PAVILION.

Bottling house at Healing Springs, early 1900s.   BCHS

Workers at the Rubino Healing Springs bottling works in the 1890s.   BCHS

The Healing Springs Hotel dining hall that later would become the Cascades Inn, late 1800s. BCHS

Cascades Inn, 1930s. Notice the difference in the front facade of the two photographs. This building is now closed. VA

Healing Springs spring-house. BCHS

Present-day remains of the Healing Springs.

The old bathhouse, now converted into a guest cottage. BCHS

CHAPTER SIX

❦ T A K I N G T H E C U R E ❧

Starting in the late 18th century, and continuing into the 19th century, health resorts, spas and baths sprung up in the Allegheny Mountains of Virginia and West Virginia. This proliferation was due mainly to the health conditions that prevailed along the Eastern Seaboard and to the primitive nature of the medical profession at the time.

The mountains provided an escape from the heat and high humidity of the lowlands; even today this is an accepted treatment for certain ailments. Yet the main drawing card for the ailing was the springs—both the hot springs and those offering mineral waters. In the Warm Springs Valley it was advertised that the springs—Warm, Hot or Healing—could cure, or at least relieve, the symptoms of diseases such as gout, rheumatism, arthritis, neuritis, lumbago, hypertension, nephritis and nervous disorders.

Whether in fact the "taking" of the waters, either externally or internally, had any lasting effect on the suffering visitor is still open to conjecture. Given the lack of sophisticated alternatives offered at the time by the medical profession, certainly there were some benefits from the use of the waters. Nor can one overlook the social aspects of life at the resorts, which also must have been of some therapeutic value.

Dr. Thomas Goode was instrumental in developing the health facilities at Hot Springs, which, until the mid-19th century, were overshadowed by the Warm Springs Spa. In the 1830s, Goode took over The Homestead and commenced to upgrade its facilities. These facilities, and others in the valley, were described by writer Peregrine Prolix in a book published in 1837 called *Letters Descriptive of the Virginia Springs:*

> *...There are two famous baths here, the Spout and the Boiler: the former is said to be preferred by Orators, the latter by Poets and Warriors. The temperature of both is about 106 Fahrenheit, a degree of heat which is a little scalding at first, but which becomes pleasant as soon as the bather is chin deep in the health-restoring fluid.*
>
> *The Spout bath is so called, because a constant stream of water is led from a hot spring through a perforated log, from the end of which (quasi spout) it pours into the bath, affording the bather an opportunity of receiving the stream upon any part of his body or limbs, into which rheumatism has thrust his uncomfortable claws. This is covered by a wooden building open at top, and has adjoining to it a dressing-room, in which is a fire. After emerging from this bath you must go to your room well wrapped up, and sit or lie until the perspiration subsides.*
>
> *The boiler is enclosed in a large wooden house which excludes the external air, and in which are ten or twelve little rooms, each containing a cot and mattress whereon to lie and perspire after leaving the bath. You remain in the bath until the big drops have started on your forehead, and begin to chase one another down your innocent nose: then you walk out of the bath into one of the little rooms previously prepared for you by the attentive and judicious superintendent, who wraps you in flannel from top to toe, yea, in toto, except the tip of your nose: then he lays upon you six blankets, and having put you in a comfortable fix, leaves you to be amused with reflection and perspiration, while he fixes the other bathers. Perspiration soon starts from every pore, and you distinctly feel it tickling and trickling down your sides. Sometimes it penetrates the blankets, mattress and sackenbottom, and streams upon the floor.*

When you have sweat enough, which will be in from thirty to ninety minutes, you call to the attendant, who comes, and removes one blanket, and at intervals of five minutes, the others one by one. Thus you are gradually cooled, and rise and dress, without the least danger of taking cold.

The effect of this bath on rheumatic and gouty affections, and on old deep-seated and chronic complaints, that medicine does not seem to reach, is very beneficial. It restores the surface to a good condition, and promotes the healthy action of the skin: and every person who drinks the water of the various sulphur springs, should afterwards stop here two to three weeks, and try the virtue of the boiler.

I remained here six days, and took the bath every day, with the best results: and the last day I bathed, a friend of mine, who had arrived in a very debilitated condition ten weeks before, was taking his seventieth bath, and had entirely recovered his health, having gained in weight nearly a pound a day.

Soda Springs springhouse is located next to the former formal gardens. This area is now the site of the South Wing and Conference Center.   BCHS

The early bathhouses built by Goode were in the vicinity of the present-day Casino. The "Pleasure Pool" was housed in a rectangular building approximately 100 feet by 25 feet divided into mens' and womens' sections. Boiler Spring, the largest of many springs in the area, supplied most of the water to the pool.

Two smaller buildings also were supplied with spring water. One, fed by Spout Spring, was used for the famous "Spout Bath" treatment. A steady stream of water was directed by a spout onto an individual's body, somewhat in the manner of a hose. This, in combination with bathing and massage, would give relief from many aches and pains. Another spring supplied water to an octagonal bathhouse called the "Plunge." Its pool is still intact in front of the present Bathhouse (Spa building).

These springs, along with others in the Hot Springs area, have been noted for their consistent temperatures. The hottest spring in the area is 106 degrees F; the coolest is 102.5 degrees F.

In 1892, the present Bathhouse (now called The Homestead Spa) was constructed, modeled somewhat after European spa buildings. It formed an integral part of the hotel complex, though it was connected to the hotel only by means of a viaduct. The new building included a solarium, casino, spout baths, tub baths and dressing rooms. In 1903 the adjacent 85- by 30-foot indoor swimming pool was built. An outdoor pool has also been constructed next to the Spa.

In the early 1900s, the Zander room was constructed in the Bathhouse. It contained workout machines developed by Dr. Gustav Zander of Sweden, who produced the forerunners of the popular gym machines used by many today.

Through the decades, thousands of people have traveled to the Warm Springs Valley seeking treatment for their ailments. Today, The Homestead still offers complete health facilities for its guests. These facilities, however, are used more for relaxation and as a relief from tension than as a cure for a particular disease.

The Soda Springs springhouse, reconstructed in 1922, was located in front of the present Conference Center. VA

Building the new Bathhouse in 1892.   BCHS

The newly completed Bathhouse in 1892 was a magnificent structure, built at a cost of $154,000. An indoor and outdoor swimming pool have since been added.

BCHS

Interior of the newly constructed Bathhouse, 1890s.   VA

The Zander Room in the Bathhouse contained a variety of weight and health-related machines. They were invented by a Swedish doctor named Zander. These machines are still in existence at the Spa. H

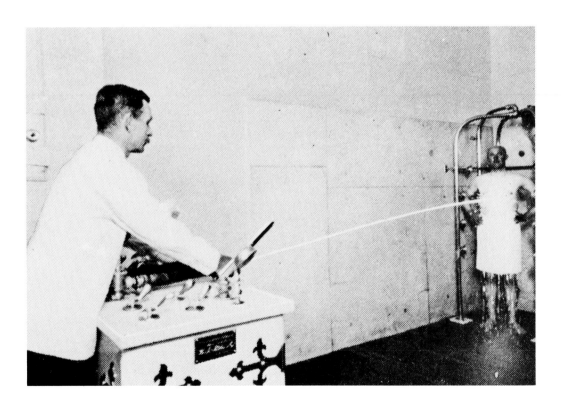

An early view of a spout bath. A steady stream of water was directed on the body with some force to relieve tension and relax the muscles. It is still in use today. H

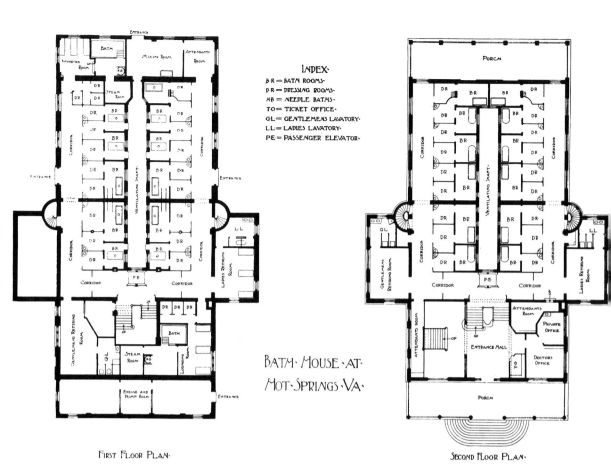

INDEX·
B·R = BATH ROOMS·
D·R = DRESSING ROOMS·
NB = NEEDLE BATHS·
T·O = TICKET OFFICE·
GL = GENTLEMENS LAVATORY·
LL = LADIES LAVATORY·
P·E = PASSENGER ELEVATOR·

BATH· HOUSE ·AT·
HOT·SPRINGS·VA·

FIRST FLOOR PLAN·

SECOND FLOOR PLAN·

The Homestead Spa as it appears today.

H

Interior of the indoor swimming pool, constructed adjacent to the Bathhouse about 1903. VHS

A portable carrying device used for invalids in the late 1800s. BCHS

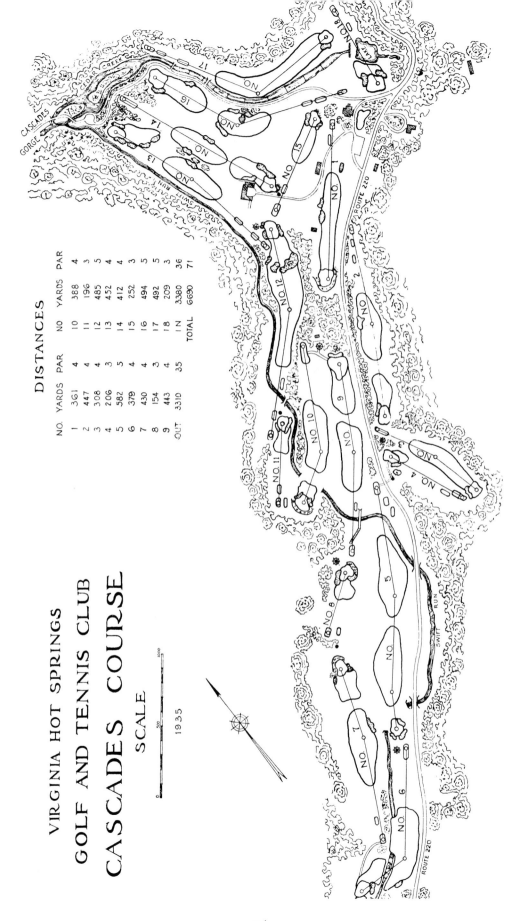

VIRGINIA HOT SPRINGS
GOLF AND TENNIS CLUB
CASCADES COURSE

SCALE

1935

DISTANCES

NO.	YARDS	PAR	NO	YARDS	PAR
1	361	4	10	388	4
2	447	4	11	196	3
3	308	4	12	485	5
4	206	3	13	452	4
5	582	5	14	412	4
6	379	4	15	252	3
7	430	4	16	494	5
8	154	3	17	492	5
9	443	4	18	209	3
OUT	3310	35	IN	3380	36
			TOTAL	6690	71

CHAPTER SEVEN

◆§ S P O R T S §◆

T he resort originally was built as a health spa, but as the fad for these facilities waned, The Homestead introduced other activities. In 1892 both golf and tennis were offered to guests.

While the game of golf originated in Scotland possibly as long as 900 years ago, it was not until 1887 that the first golf club was established in the United States. The course at the Homestead was constructed just five years later. The first tee of this primitive course is the oldest tee in continuous use in this country.

In 1899 the Virginia Hot Springs Golf and Tennis Club was formed and the first "professional" golfer, Herbert A.C. Beauclerk, was hired. With a six-hole course, The Homestead now was definitely in the golf business. The course continued to grow, without real planning, and eventually professional help was brought in to lay out the 18-hole Homestead Course, which is still in existence today.

Later, a small course was constructed in an upland pasture, now the site of the ski area. This was originally called the "goat course" and was later used by hotel employees.

By the early 1920s, the single nine-hole Homestead Course was not adequate for the number of guests using it and the resort decided to expand its golfing facilities.

The Virginia Hot Springs Co. purchased the Rubino land, just down the road from Hot Springs at Healing Springs. This land, in addition to several adjacent farms, became the site of the present-day Cascades Course. The magnificent Rubino home located on the property was taken over as a clubhouse and is still in use today. Upon its opening in 1924, the course immediately became very popular. It has been the site of numerous national tournaments.

A third course, the Lower Cascades, was constructed in 1963. Designed by the well-known golf course architect Robert Trent Jones, it is a 6,726-yard, par-72 course. The Cascades Course is 6,566 yards, par-70.

The first tennis court was built in 1892 on the lawn near the front entrance of the hotel and in 1894 three courts were built next to the Casino. Five more were built in the early 1930s and 11 more since then.

Other sports facilities at the resort include a trap and skeet range, riding stables, an eight-lane bowling alley, two lawn-bowling courts, an outdoor children's playground, one indoor and two outdoor swimming pools and stocked Rainbow trout streams.

Teeing-off at the first tee of The Homestead Course, early 1900s. Constructed in 1892, this is the oldest original tee of one of the oldest golf courses in the United States.   BCHS

View of the Cascades Club and golf course site in 1893. At this time the Thompson farm property consisted of a mill and surrounding cottages. It was purchased in 1923 along with the Rubino property for the new Cascades Course.　　　BCHS

This early-day fifth-wheeler, shown circa 1930, transported golfers from The Homestead to the Cascades Course.　　　H

Cascades Course.   VA

1928 golf tournament at the Cascades Course.   VA

Champion Glenna Collett Vare receives her trophy.   VA

Sam Snead has been a household name in the golfing community for the past four decades. A few years ago, after an illustrious career at The Greenbrier in West Virginia, Snead returned to his birthplace and to the beloved mountains of Bath County. He is now on the staff at The Homestead.

Snead was born in 1912, the fifth of five sons of Laura and Harry Snead. The elder Snead worked in the hotel's powerhouse. Sam grew up sneaking onto the old nine-hole golf course, but he did not get to play the regulation 18-hole course until he was in high school. He did not take to books very well, but golf and other athletics became second nature to him. In the 1930s, after high school, he turned down college to become an assistant pro at The Homestead.

Having grown up in a family that didn't have much money, Snead had a lot of catching up to do to perfect his golf game and enter the large-purse tournaments. He finished third in his first big tournament, the Cascades Open, in 1935, and several other tournaments that year put him on the road to a career that is still unmatched in golf history.

In 1936, Snead became teaching pro at The Homestead, but he made very little money. The manager of the Greenbrier, Freddie Martin, lured Snead to his resort later that year, and Snead's income almost immediately doubled. He was beginning to make a name for himself on the golf circuit and by the middle of the year he had signed a contract with Wilson Sporting Goods. He became the second biggest money winner of 1936; by 1938 he was the top money winner with a record $20,000.

Snead's name would become synonymous with golf for the next 40 years. Although he played the major tournaments at a time when purses were much smaller than today, he has amassed a spectacular record: winner of the P.G.A. three times; three-time winner of the Masters; named player-of-the-year in 1949; elected to the Hall of Fame in 1953; leading money winner in 1938, 1949 and 1950; member of the Ryder Cup team eight times and captain in 1959 and 1969; has 20 more tournament victories than any other golfer in P.G.A. history; the first golfer ever to break a score of 60 in P.G.A. competition; four-time winner of the Vardon Trophy for the lowest scoring average during the year; record for the lowest scoring average in one year (69.23 in 96 rounds in 1950); and the record for most victories in one P.G.A. event (eight victories in the Greater Greensboro Open).

Snead also won the first P.G.A. Legends of Golf Tournament for players over 50. He was 66 years old at the time. He won it again in 1982 when he was just one month short of his 70th birthday.

Today Snead lives in a very spacious home on the old Snead homestead near the Cascades Course. He still takes an active interest in the resort's golf business.

CHAPTER EIGHT

U ntil the late 1950s, The Homestead would nearly close up during the winter season, when outside activities were severely limited by the cold weather of the Allegheny Mountains. But the weather and the mountains were to work to the resort's advantage when an enterprising Austrian named Sepp Kober showed up at the hotel one spring.

A former member of the German Alpine troops, Kober became prominent in European ski circles after World War II. He coached the Norwegian and Spanish ski teams in the early 1950s, and directed several ski schools on the Continent. In 1957 he moved to the well-known ski resort at Stowe, Vt., and the next season wound up at a little area in Tucker County, W. Va., called Cabin Mountain.

In 1959 he came to The Homestead and proceeded to convert an old golf course into the South's first real ski area and was the first to use the recently developed snow gun to produce man-made snow. When the ski area opened in December of that year, it featured an unusual uphill trestle-car system, similar to the one constructed in the 1930s at Mount Cranmore in New Hampshire. This piece of engineering, along with the snow gun, transformed The Homestead into a year-round resort.

Kober, and the winter facilities he developed, which include an Olympic-size ice rink, are among the South's finest, and Kober is known throughout the ski industry as the "father of Southern skiing." The Homestead Ski Area has now grown to five slopes, novice to expert; three trails, intermediate to expert; a double chairlift; T-bar; and two rope tows. It has a base elevation of 2,500 feet and a vertical drop of 700 feet.

Sepp Kober in 1959. Kober, under the direction of The Homestead's president, Thomas J. Lennon, converted a golf course into the South's first ski area. H

From 1959 to 1980 this trestle system hauled skiers to the top of the main ski run. H

A chairlift now transports skiers to the top. H

Winter sunbathers enjoy a view of the ski slopes. The Olympic-size ice rink is in the background. H

Sepp Kober, left, and Howard Head, right, at The Homestead ski area, 1960s. Head developed the first metal ski. H

CHAPTER NINE

War had touched the Warm Springs Valley once before when troops of the Confederate Army had used hotel buildings as a hospital and rest area. Now, some 80 years later, the valley again felt the effects of war, although this time the actual scene of the conflict was in far-off Europe and Asia.

With the attack on Pearl Harbor in December 1941, the entire country went on a war footing, and The Homestead did not escape involvement. On Dec. 18, 1941, the hotel management received a phone call from the State Department requesting the use of the hotel's facilities for the internment of Axis diplomats who had been caught in this country when the U.S. entered the war. The caller suggested that the government probably would use the hotel whether the management agreed or not.

In accordance with international law, these diplomats were to be granted humane treatment—the same treatment the United States hoped would be given to its nationals in Germany, Italy and Japan. Thus a comfortable but secure location was desired; the Homestead could provide both. While the Germans, Italians and other European nationals were sent to The Greenbrier, in White Sulphur Springs, W.Va., the Japanese were to be sent to The Homestead.

There was no indication how long the Japanese were to be kept at the hotel. Just before the diplomats' arrival, all remaining guests were asked to leave and all bookings were cancelled. Approximately 60 Border Patrolmen were assigned to The Homestead to act as security guards; the entire complex was to be guarded day and night. Only authorized personnel and hotel employees were allowed in the hotel, and all employees were investigated by the FBI before the diplomats arrived.

In total, 334 people were held in the hotel, with the first 67 arriving on Dec. 29. The Japanese were not allowed to communicate with anyone on the outside, and their mail was meticulously censored. While they were permitted access to most of the hotel, they could not at first go into the theater and they were never allowed in The Homestead Club. Most sports activities were denied to them, including use of the Spa, although later they were allowed access to that facility. United States officials did not want to give the Japanese any greater privileges than were accorded the U.S. diplomats interned in Tokyo.

Never was there any real trouble between the Japanese and the hotel management and staff or the Border Patrolmen. But, on a few occasions, when the Japanese learned of a great victory such as the capture of Singapore, they would delight in making note of it. This patriotism was not universal, however. Some of the internees had lived in the United States for many years and professed no desire to be repatriated to Japan.

Operations ran smoothly through the winter of 1942, but the hotel management was anxious to open the hotel to regular guests with the coming spring season. Hotel expenses for the Japanese were paid by the government, but the internment was certainly never a money-making experience for the hotel company, and financial losses would be great if the internees were not moved by spring. The hotel was still suffering from the effects of the Depression years.

After much investigation, in late March it was decided to move all the Japanese to The Greenbrier. An extensive clean-up removed all traces of the recent visitors and the hotel was ready for business on Easter Sunday. But only five guests showed up, and it took a few weeks to gain back the pre-war clientele.

Due to the sensitive nature of the three-month incarceration, no photographs were allowed and only a written record remains of this phase of the hotel's history.

Other foreigners were interned in the Warm Springs Valley later in the war. In 1943, the State Department leased the Three Hills resort at Warm Springs, where the Vichy French were interned. Soon the French were moved to the Cascades Inn, a less isolated site. The French stay was relatively short, and it was not marked by the close confinement that was necessary for the Japanese at The Homestead.

Japanese Ambassador Nomura and Special Envoy Kurusu are shown leaving the White House about Nov. 26, 1941, after receiving rejections on proposals that they had hoped would avert war. The two diplomats were interned at The Homestead.

National Archives

Delegates from Allied nations are arriving at the Hot Springs railroad station for a United Nations Food Conference held at The Homestead in May 1943.

UPI/Bettmann Newsphotos

Indoor pool next to the Spa building.

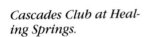

Cascades Club at Healing Springs.

The Women's Pool and Bathhouse, Warm Springs.

Bird's-eye View of the Homestead.   Hot Springs, Va.

A 1917 view of The Homestead.

The Great Hall, 1908.

The Bathhouse, 1912.

Warm Springs Hotel, 1911.

Cascades Inn, Healing Springs, 1930s.

Rubino's house at Healing Springs, now the Cascades Club.

Front entrance to The Homestead.

North view of The Homestead showing the Casino, tennis court and first tee of The Homestead Course.

The Great Hall.

The Japanese Room, 1915.

The Billiard Room, 1915.

The Ballroom, 1915.

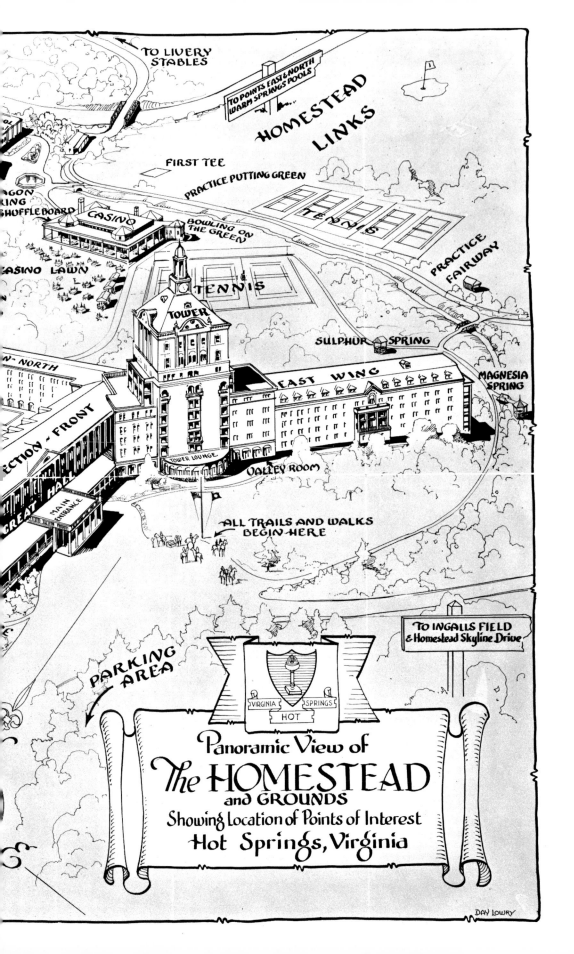

Panoramic View of
The HOMESTEAD
and GROUNDS
Showing Location of Points of Interest
Hot Springs, Virginia

Military guards at the United Nations Food Conference in May 1943.

FAMOUS VISITORS

FAMOUS VISITORS 1940s

Cordell Hull, Secretary of State from 1937-1944 and a proponent of the creation of the United Nations in 1945.

James Byrnes and wife. Byrnes was a U.S. Supreme Court justice, headed several government agencies during World War II and Secretary of State in 1945.

Ex-governor of New York and 1944 presidential candidate, Thomas Dewey and aides.

Famous movie actor Van Johnson.

Heavyweight boxing champion Gene Tunney and his wife.

Left to right: Walter J. Touhy, chairman of the C&O Railroad, and his wife; U.S. Supreme Court Justice Fred Vinson and his wife; and French Ambassador Bonnet and his wife at the Hot Springs railroad station, 1947.